A Visual Compendium Of Hospital Records

Written, compiled and edited by Ricky Trickartt and Chris Goss

NHS200: A Visual Compendium of Hospital Records

Written, compiled and edited by Ricky Trickartt and Chris Goss.
Designed by Ricky Trickartt.

First edition.

Published by Hospital Records Limited.

ISBN: 978-0-9570965-0-9

NHS200 © Hospital Records Limited 2011.

Printed in the UK.
Typeset in Berthold Akzidenz Grotesk.

Hospital Records Limited
The Purple Gates
182-184 Dartmouth Road
London
SE26 4QZ

WWW.HOSPITALRECORDS.COM

When Chris and Ricky decided they needed a foreword for this book they turned to me, head of promo for Hospital Records, as apparently my job means I'm in charge of "writing stuff" for the label. So here we go...

When I was at school in the backwoods of East Anglia in the mid '90s, I became obsessed by the new sounds I was hearing from the big bad city. I loved the music, but I hated all the plastic gangsta posturing which seemed to be part and parcel of it at the time - all puffa jackets and gold chains. With the D+B scene exploding, I was drawn to the music on the edge of the genre, and tunes like "Song In The Key Of Knife" and "Pull The Plug" sounded totally ground-breaking to my ears. When I made my weekly pilgrimage to Soundclash Records in Norwich, there was something unique and inspiring about Hospital twelve inches which jumped out from the racks. The sleeves on crisp white board with their die-cut H logo, the hand-printed prescription labels, the pun-tastic titles all added up to something special; they made you prick up your ears, and stood out from the dodgy 3D computer graphics which were the lingua franca of D+B imagery at the time.

When I made my way to London and finally got my foot in the Red Corner Door, I was surprised to find a tiny operation (no pun intended) lay behind. Spending happy hours sticking those hallowed stickers on promo 12"s and making tea, I became fully infected with the Hospital bug. Fast forward over a decade, and to say I'm proud of where we've got to doesn't quite sum it up. From hand-printed stickers to topping the iTunes chart; from tiny Shoreditch sweat boxes to worldwide events and capacity crowds at Brixton Academy; along the way it's all been done with the same love and belief that Tony and Chris put in at the start. This book attempts to chart some of that journey visually, and some of the friends we've made along the way.

Tom Kelsey
Hospital Records
November 2011

Hospital Logo

Hospital Font
Eurostile Bold Extended 2

Small text:
Berthold Akzidenz Grotesk

Colours:
White, Black and Pantone 291 (Sky Blue)

Building
(1996)

Med School
(2006)

College Seal
(2011)

Exploded
(Brixton 2011)

Emergency Medical
Service (2001)

Shatter
(2008)

Songs In The Key
Of Knife (2008)

Transmitter
(2008)

Cripples
(1998)

War On Vinyl
(2008)

Overlay
(Brixton 2010)

Jungle Music
(2009)

Pull The Plug
(1998)

Hospital Podcast
(2006)

Weapons 3
(2007)

Panda
(2007)

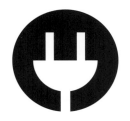

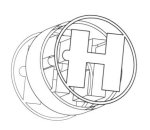

jungle
music

early releases

Throughout Hospital's history, the housebag has been an integral part of the label's identity. Ever since the first release (pictured left), vinyl singles have been delivered in a clinical white die-cut sleeve, complete with prescription label (see over).

Later versions of the housebag had the H perforated instead of die-cut, leaving DJs wondering whether they were meant to punch the H out or leave it intact. The last Hospital single to use the housebag before moving on to 100% full artwork was Nu:Tone's 'Breathless' in 2004.

The perforations were brought back for 2008's 'Classic Symptoms' reissue series. These sleeves featured a misprint that was misinterpreted for stitches.

Also pictured are the centre labels for the first three releases. The label has come a long way from these sometimes gruesome close-ups of surgery!

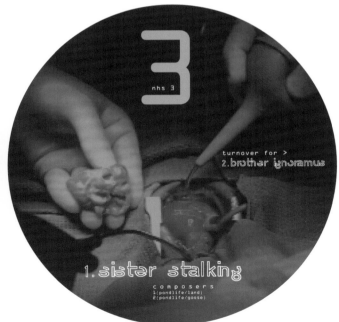

prescriptions

The details are what make the identity, and since the very first release in 1996, prescription labels have been printed for every record by the same company since NHS1 - Cee Gee Agencies.

It's still going strong today - a vintage (and now very yellow) Macintosh and its accompanying ImageWriter are still maintained and in working order at The Purple Gates.

Since moving to full artwork sleeves for our records, the labels may not go on every single release, but they do still make it onto all of our white-label test pressings and promos!

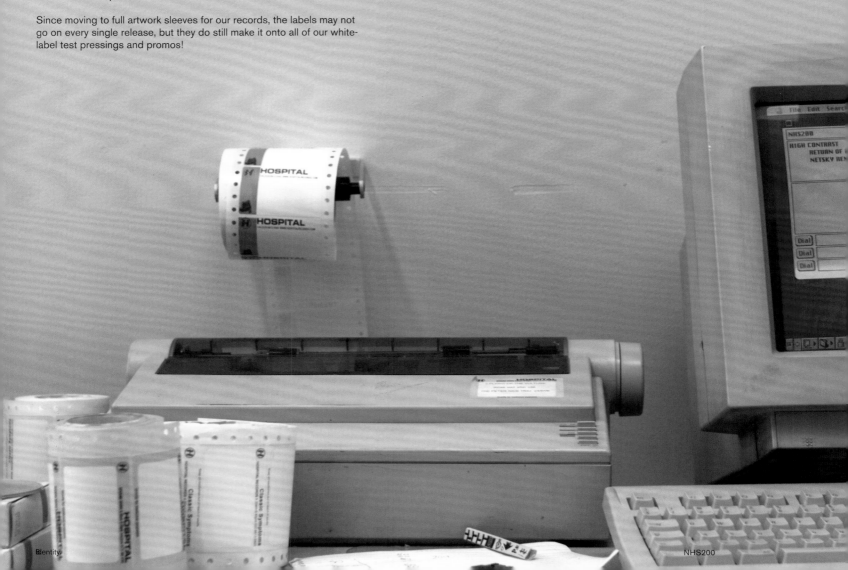

casualty

Hospital's short-lived trip-hop twin sister emerged at the same time. Only one could survive, and that turned out to be Hospital.

hospickle
red corner door
17 barons court road
London
W14 9DP

barons court

Our first home was out West, a corner property with red doors.

Barons Court

Barons Court Studio in the heyday of outboard equipment

Barons Court

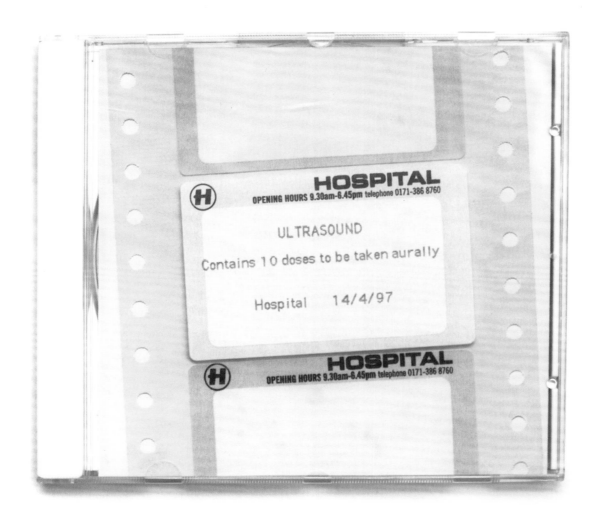

HOSPITAL
OPENING HOURS 9.30am-6.45pm telephone 0171-386 8760

ULTRASOUND

Contains 10 doses to be taken aurally

Hospital   14/4/97

HOSPITAL
OPENING HOURS 9.30am-6.45pm telephone 0171-386 8760

14

ultrasound

Hospital's fourth release was the first long player.

In keeping with the vinyl sleeve designs, even this first CD was stickered with a prescription label.

The first proper press shot was taken at Yo Sushi! in Soho by Adrian Fisk, for a full page Mixmag feature in 1997.

japan

In 1998, Sony Japan went mad and started licensing all kinds of
Drum+Bass in from the UK, including a lot of Hospital content. With the
backing of a major label, Tony and Chris went to Japan, where they got
to lark around in full medical gear in a decomissioned medical hospital
turned TV set.

Between Chris and Japanese design studio TGB, some very unique
artwork and packaging was created.

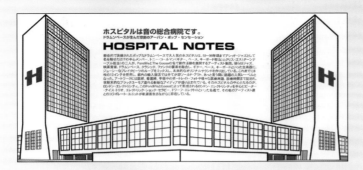

ホスピタルは音の総合病院です。

ドラム・ベースが生んだ驚異のアーバン・ポップ・センセーション

HOSPITAL NOTES

都会的で洗練されたアップなドラム・ベースで人気のホスピタルは、93〜96年頃までアシッド・ジャズとして名を馳せたロリの中心メンバー、トニー・コールマン(ギター、ベース、キーボード担当)とクリス・ゴス(ターンテーブル担当)の二人が、Parallel/The Gossel)を下で制作活動を展開するアーティスト集団。

映画音楽、ドラム・ベース、クラシック、ファンクの要素を融合し、ギター、ベース、キーボードといった生楽器で、ジャジーなブレイク・ビーツのループをミックス。未来的なアンダーグラウンドを作り出している。これまでに作った13インチを発売、店頭の購入意欲ではすぐに売りソールド・アウト、あっと言う間に即完の人気レコードとなった。アートワーク面には医師、看護婦、病室での女性のエレベーター、フォトや得られた医療映像、診療映画で写された世界末的なブラック・ユーモアと斬新なアイディア分部り込まれている。そのホスピタルの中心人たちものが、ロンドン・エレクトリシティ、CDのPandit(alとGossel)によって形成されたロンドン・エレクトリシティを中心とするピーター・ナイス・トリオ、エレクトリック・ショック・セラピー、ドワーフ・エレクトロといった名義で、その他のアーティスト達とコラポレート・ユニット分楽器演奏を互なからに存在している。

Ultrasound was Hospital's first trip across the Pacific. The Japanese
edition came in a CD-sized version of the classic Hospital cut-out sleeve.

Ever wondered why the Plastic Surgery series appeared to start at 2?

The first edition was a Japan-exclusive product; a collection of early Hospital outings reworked by some of our Japanese compadres. The packaging included a heat-sealed plastic sleeve for the three-piece vinyl release and a rather nice CD package.

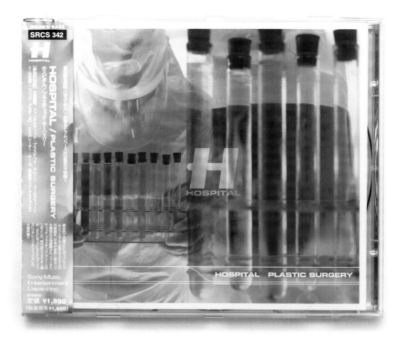

HOSPITAL PLASTIC SURGERY

HOSPITAL

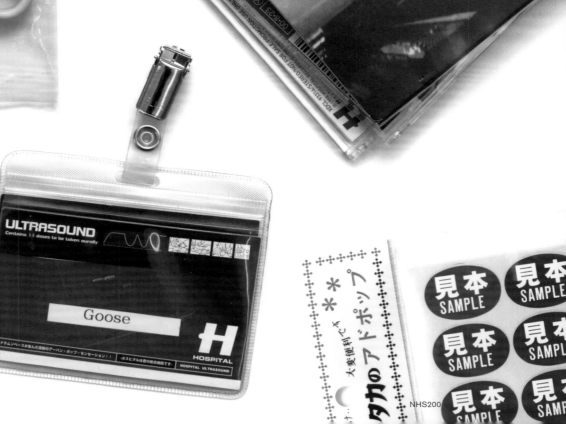

More beats and pieces from Hospital in Japan.

The yellow plug is in fact a Japanese adaptor into which you can plug devices that are otherwise tricky to 'pull'. The perfect promo device!

NHS200

The Office One crew from Japan, led by Toru Nihonghi, were so very good at the details. For the launch of Ultrasound, they produced a number of mini medical bags, complete with full first-aid supplies and Hospital stickers.

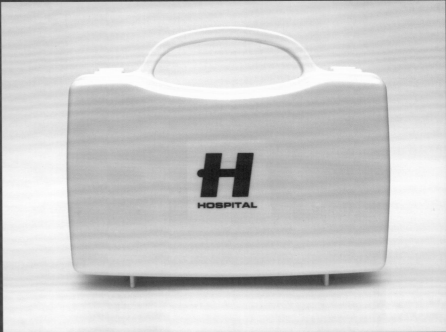

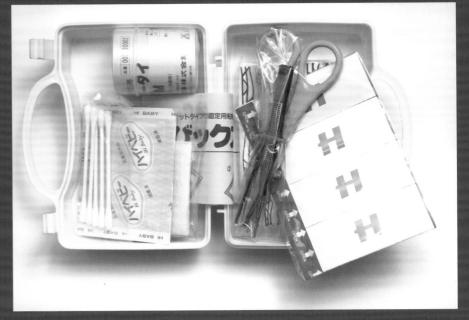

pull the plug

The first full artist album featured a snapshot portrait from Fiona Freund, taken in an empty Richmond hospital. Launch party invites were generally thrown away, since plenty of our friends assumed they were genuine red bills chasing payment.

london elektricity

pull the plug launch party
Thurs 03 June 9.30pm The Annexe, Soho W1

Telephone us on **0171 386 8760**
send us a fax on **0171 381 8014**
or e-mail us info@hospitalrecords.com

HOSPITAL

03/06/99

LONDON ELEKTRICITY "PULL THE PLUG"
NHS12CD   barcode: 666017002224

LONDON ELEKTRICITY "PULL THE PLUG"
NHS12CDX   barcode: 666017003122

LONDON ELEKTRICITY "PULL THE PLUG"
NHS12LP   barcode: 666017002217

Reminder *launch party*

If you have recently decided to come to this launch party, then accept our thanks and apologies for having troubled you. If not, please make a date in your diary immediately. Failure to do so may result in musical dissatisfaction and clinical unhappiness.

On Thursday 3rd June at The Annexe, 1 Dean Street, Soho, W1
Hospital Records present the launch party for
London Elektricity's album PULL THE PLUG:

deejays

Marcus DA INTALLEX (Galaxy 102) / Dj ADDICTION (Swerve)
Chris GOSS & Tony COLMAN (London Elektricity)
DJ Klaus (Main Source/Octagon)
Pete HERBERT (Atlas Records)
plus a special 'one-off' performance by
London ELEKTRICITY
featuring Lianne Carrol, Landmass & Pete Shrubshall

sneaky visual stimuli courtesy the Light Surgery

timing:

9.30pm until 2.30am - by invitation / otherwise £5 door charge

info/list - Main Source 0171 371 7997 :: Hospital 0171 386 8760
venue info - The Annexe 1 Dean St, Soho, W1 0171 287 960 8

pull the plug

www.hospitalrecords.com

⇉ The 'Plug vinyl release followed
on from the housebag design with
another die-cut sleeve

london elektricity
PULL THE PLUG

From the launch party at The Annexe, with a logo box made from an old Coke sign discarded by our local off-licence.

out patients

Hospital's eclectic electric was inspired by a Mr Scruff remix swap, and grew into our first exclusive compilation project.

double CD

out patients ^(H)

jazz breaks, future soul & drum+bass

15 exclusive new tracks:: including aquasky, marcus intalex + s.t. files
london elektricity, skitz + julie dexter, mc mello & mr scruff

double CD : disc 2 mixed by landslide

out patients 2 ^(H)

future jazz & 2-step soul

exclusive new music from **audiomontage**
future homosapiens : jazztronik : les gammas
landslide : london elektricity : pulcinella
solid roots : swell session : yukihiro fukutomi

The vinyl LP comprised three 12" and one 10", as well as a doublepack 12" vinyl promo, a one-sided 12" single and a 7" single. The flyers were modelled on Chris' NHS medical card.

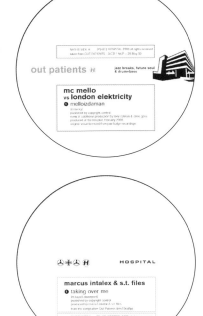

This is your
NHS medical card
Please keep it in a safe place. It is proof that you are entitled to NHS treatment.
Your NHS number is
020 7386 8760

Your local Health Authority is

HOSPITAL
17 Barons Court Road
London W14 9DP

www.hospitalrecords.com

out patient
details here

To the patient

Please read the notes about this album
on the other side of this card
You will be able to purchase this album
in all good retailers from 29 May 2000

If you are not the patient, as named
above, please fill out your details below
and return to Hospital

Take note of the following appointments

10 June	**Off Centre**	333, London
16 June	**CD Presents**	Thekla, Bristol
17 June	**Phonic Hoop**	Enigma, Brighton
24 June	**Futuristica**	Cuba, Edinburgh
01 July	**Sonic Mook**	Scala, London
05 July	**Jelly Jazz**	Quay Club, Plymouth

Postcode

E-mail

out patients ^(R)
jazz breaks, future soul & drum+bass

OUT
PATIENTS
THREE HOSPITAL

The Out Patients series finished with Volume Three, featuring some great artwork from Snorre Seim (Sesong). Its release gave way very nicely to Phuturistix, who not only feaured on OP3 but went on to release their album 'Feel It Out' on Hospital the same year. The Gry Garness cover photo features the hands of Chris, Tom, Brian, Nigel and...

zed bias+injekta present

phuturisti4
Featuring Jenna G

beautiful
b/w
bugz
in the
attic
remix

zed bias+injekta present

phuturisti4
Featuring Jenna G

beautiful
remixed by
**london
elektricity
+
nu:tone**

...Tony's gold Hospital sygnet
ring, made by Chris' jewellery
designer wife, Sally.

Out Patients and Phuturistix

landslide

Hospital's first signing came in the shape of Tim Land, AKA Landslide.

His album included an ode to his golden Vauxhall Cavalier and an exploration of more BPMs and styles than would've been considered acceptable in 2000.

Still a friend of Hospital, Landslide invented Rainbow Grime and can now be found occasionally re-recording vocals for the label's new whipper-snappers and wrangling with lots of children.

The back cover of 'Drum and Bossa'
is emblazoned with the quote "*very
tasty...like chips with mayonnaise it
shouldn't work but it does*"; courtesy
of Jockey Slut.

That says it all really!

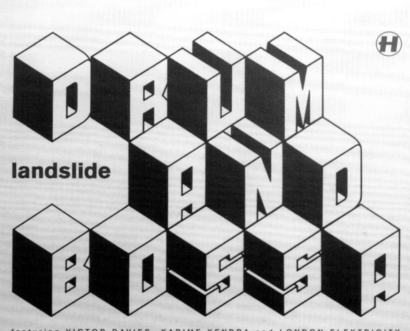

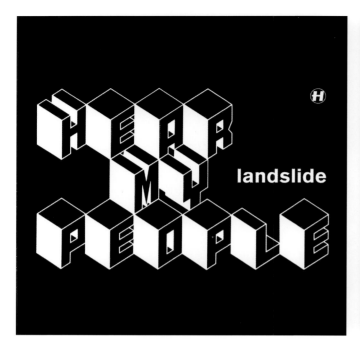

landslide

FILE UNDER:
2-step garage
/ jazz-breaks

hospital : here to help
(removable sticker)

...These stickers never really worked

LANDSLIDE
+ ALISON CROCKETT
IT'S NOT OVER

SIDE A. 45RPM

Landslide found his home
inventing new sub-genres, much
to the confusion of the masses.
After a variety of remixes across
the label, his last single with
Hospital was the aptly titled
'It's Not Over', featuring Alison
Crockett.

We still love Landslide, we just
wish he'd make more music!

danny byrd
❶ do it again
(byrd)
published by songs in the key of knife/westbury music
produced & arranged by danny byrd
recorded & mixed at the eastfield, bath

NHS22 SIDE A   [P]+[C] HOSPITAL 2000 all rights reserved

delta
submerged

nhs

landslide featuring **karime kendra**
❶ down down
(land/kendra)
published by songs in the key of knife/westbury music
produced by tim land at sunrise studios, acton town
mixed by tony colman & tim land at hospital

NHS21 SIDE A   [P]+[C] HOSPITAL 2000 all rights reserved

danny byrd featuring **somniare**
❶ changes
(d.byrd/d.thomas)
published by songs in the key of knife/westbury music
produced by danny byrd. vocals by somniare
vocals written by d.byrd/d.thomas

NHS27 SIDE A   [P]+[C] HOSPITAL 2001 all rights reserved

NHS42 :: A :: [P]+[C] HOSPITAL / TONGUE+GROOVE 2002

danny byrd
changes
calibre remix

written by d.byrd & d.thomas. vocals: somniare
remixed by calibre, courtesy of creative source
published by songs in the key of knife/westbury music
taken from the forthcoming compilation

plastic surgery ³

landslide featuring **london elektricity**
❶ incurable voices
(land/colman)
published by songs in the key of knife/westbury music
produced by tim land at sunrise studios, acton town
from the debut album "Drum&Bossa" - out 16.10.00

NHS24 SIDE A   [P]+[C] HOSPITAL 2000 all rights reserved

plastic surgery ²

carlito + addiction
❶ the ride
written & produced by carlito + addiction
published by copyright control
engineered by james eelson-wade; recorded in the diffusion room
taken from the compilation 'plastic surgery' - released 16.04.01

NHS29 SIDE A   [P]+[C] HOSPITAL 2001 all rights reserved

dagga
laughing gas

SIDE A. 45RPM
WRITTEN & PRODUCED BY LUKE FERRIS.
PUBLISHED BY SONGS IN THE KEY OF KNIFE
/ WESTBURY MUSIC
RECORDED AT INDIKA STUDIOS.

ALL RIGHTS RESERVED. MADE IN ENGLAND.
[P]+[C] HOSPITAL / TONGUE+GROOVE 2002.

nhs45 www.hospitalrecords.com

plastic surgery

...returned to Hospital in the UK in 2001 with Volume Two, a collection of tracks from the then-exploding liquid Drum+Bass scene, including the first track to ever be released from Welsh wunderkind High Contrast.

Along with the music came some of Hospital's most classic artwork. Volume Two's cover was adorned by a paediatric operating table donated to Hospital by some early fans, Medicus Maximus in Westcliff-On-Sea. The table now has a home in Hospital's studio at The Purple Gates, where it has been serving as the most unique DJ table you are likely to see!

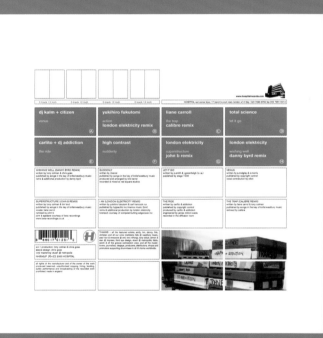

This cover taught Ricky Trickartt everything he needed to know about grid-based design principals, with a not-so-subtle nod made back to it on the sleeve of 2009's Sick Music:

TOTAL SCIENCE
ORIGIN UNKNOWN
CARLITO + ADDICTION
CALIBRE
LONDON ELEKTRICITY
DANNY BYRD
HIGH CONTRAST
DJ KALM + CITIZEN
JOHN B

The series' third instalment from 2002 was graced with, well, plastic surgery; Playmobil figures picked up while on tour in Japan.

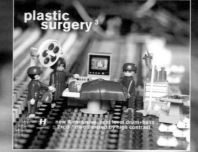

plastic
surgery³

new & exclusive, next level drum+bass
:: 2xcd / disc 2 mixed by high contrast

nitin sawhney sunset london elektricity remix
mathematics feelin
virtual suspects featuring gwen m 'crae gotta have your love
blue sonix featuring gary bardouille understand
xploding plastix treat me mean, i need the reputation
total science flip flop
tony colman synthetic
quartz your love
high contrast fooFa gold
delta love tribe
danny byrd changes calibre remix

disc 2 : 14-track mix by HIGH CONTRAST also includes:

tomahawk milkshake
delta roots
high contrast blue muse

NHS43CD
Contents as shown
Contents * Contenido
Contenuto * Innehält

HOSPITAL RECORDS LTD
THE PURPLE GATES
123-124 DARTMOUTH ROAD
LONDON SE26 4QZ
ENGLAND
www.hospital-records.com

plastic surgery 4
2x12 : DKAY+DJ LEE / ZED BIAS / CYANTIFIC / TOMAHAWK

#01

NHSS1 : BRAND NEW+EXCLUSIVE DRUM+BASS PRESSURE

plastic surgery 4
3x12 : HIGH CONTRAST / INFLUX UK / ZERO TOLERANCE
DJ KALM+CITIZEN FEAT. ADAM M / SYNCOPIX / UTAH JAZZ

#02

6660170534127. NEW AND EXCLUSIVE DRUM+BASS PRESSURE

Plastic Surgery signed off in 2003 with Volume Four, rolling in a Hospital Mercedes worthy of an African dictator. The car bonnet badge was made by Sally. Photos of Tony's beloved 3-door classic car were taken outside Herbal in Shoreditch.

The series now exists in the digital bundle 'Final Reconstruction', containing all the tracks from the series and with new artwork mashing up Volumes Two and Three.

plastic
surgery:
final reconstruction

LONDON
ELEK
TRICITY
CUM
DANCING

Klute
PART OF ME

high contrast
full intention

SIDE B :: 45RPM [P]+[C] HOSPITAL 2001
written & produced by link barrett
published by songs in the key of knife/westbury music
recorded at red square studios
all rights reserved. made in england
www.hospitalrecords.com

nhs 34

high contrast
make it tonight

SIDE A :: 45RPM [P]+[C] HOSPITAL 2001
written & produced by link barrett
published by songs in the key of knife/westbury music
recorded at red square studios
all rights reserved. made in england
www.hospitalrecords.com

nhs 37

hello penarth!

Following his debut release on the Plastic Surgery series,
a very young and mild-mannered Welshman with the alias
'High Contrast' joined the label.

RETURN OFFOREVER > JOHN B REMIX

(H) 45 RPM ::B::

written & produced by link barrett. recorded & mixed at red square studios, penarth. remixed by john b, courtesy beta recordings. (www.john-b.com). published by songs in the key of knife / westbury music. NHS44 [P]+[C] HOSPITAL / TONGUE+GROOVE 2002. all rights of the manufacturer and of the owner of the work produced reserved. unauthorised copying, hiring, lending, public performance and broadcasting of the recorded work prohibited. MADE IN ENGLAND

RETURN OFFOREVER > LANDSLIDE REMIX

(H) 45 RPM ::AA::

written & produced by lincoln barrett. recorded & mixed at red square studios, penarth. remixed by landslide at port 55, kings cross. published by songs in the key of knife / westbury music. NHS44R [P]+[C] HOSPITAL / TONGUE+GROOVE 2002. all rights of the manufacturer and of the owner of the work produced reserved. unauthorised copying, hiring, lending, public performance and broadcasting of the recorded work prohibited. MADE IN ENGLAND

HIGHCONTRAST > GLOBALLOVE

(H) 45 RPM ::A::

written by lincoln barrett / antonio carlos jobim / vinicius de moraes. published by songs in the key of knife / westbury music / campidoglio edizioni musicali. contains samples from "agua de beber" (jobim / de moraes). published by campidoglio edizioni musicali. used by permission. produced by lincoln barrett. recorded & mixed at red square studios, penarth. NHS44 [P]+[C] HOSPITAL / TONGUE + GROOVE 2002 all rights of the manufacturer and of the owner of the work produced reserved. unauthorised copying, hiring, lending, public performance and broadcasting of the recorded work prohibited. MADE IN ENGLAND

GLOBALLOVE > CALIBRE REMIX

(H) 45 RPM ::A::

written by lincoln barrett/ antonio carlos jobim / vinicius de moraes. published by songs in the key of knife / westbury music / campidoglio edizioni musicali. contains samples from "agua de beber" (jobim / de moraes). published by campidoglio edizioni musicali. used by permission. remixed by calibre, courtesy of creative source. NHS44R [P]+[C] HOSPITAL / TONGUE + GROOVE 2002 all rights of the manufacturer and of the owner of the work produced reserved. unauthorised copying, hiring, lending, public performance and broadcasting of the recorded work prohibited. MADE IN ENGLAND

High Contrast singles, 2002-3

HIGHCON TRAST>R ETURNOF FOREVER NHS40

HIGHCON TRAST>G LOBALLO VE NHS44

HIGHCONTRAST
GLOBALL OVE>CALLI BREREMIX NHS44R

HIGHCONTRAST
MUSICIS EVERYTH ING
INFLUXDATUM UK + DANNYBYRD REMIXES

NHS200

↑↑ Special Edition

↑↑ Album Launches were held in Black Market, Soho, and Catapult Records, Cardiff (Lincoln's previous workplace).

hospitality at herbal

Over six years in residency at the iconic Shoreditch sweatbox.

Herbal's initial response to our enquiries was "we don't really do drum and bass". But in October 2001, Hospitality launched as a monthly label residency at the 2-floor Shoreditch venue, with an early 'no-MC' policy. The first flyer was an appointment card, inside a sealed envelope.

APPOINTMENT CARD

HOSPITALITY

We examined you today and advise that you should refrain from work

on .... **Friday 19 October, from 9pm - 2am** ....
for the following treatment :

quality drum & bass played through a Wattco XXL system from our own specialists -
London Elektricity, High Contrast & DJ Elle

with live vocals from ...**Liane Carrol & guests**.............

plus an alternative selection of sonic remedies in the upstairs bar courtesy of -
Landslide, Swell Session & Alan Brown

charges on the night : **£5.00 or £3.00 before 10.30pm**

> **HERBAL**
> 12-14 Kingsland Road, Shoreditch, London E2 020 7613 4462
> (3 minutes walk under the bridge around the corner from 333, and the Town Hall)

NOTE TO PATIENT the first 50 paying patients on the night will receive an exclusive Hospital mix cd.

NOTES TO THE PATIENT

HOSPITALITY is the new monthly residency from Hospital Records;

> 1. at Herbal on the 3rd Friday of every month, featuring deejays and artists from the Hospital crew. We will promote the new wave of deep and soulful drum& bass, alongside alternative breakbeat flavours like 2-step and future jazz musics.

> 2. the system at Herbal is designed to make quality music sound even better; loud music doesn't have to hurt.

> 3. we will be working with vocalists to bring something extra to the club environment; don't be afraid.

the next appointments will be ...**Friday 16 November & Friday 21 December**...

§ Hospital releases this Autumn and Winter are:

24.09.01	London Elektricity vs Robert Owens "My Dreams remixes"	:nhs35
15.10.01	Landslide "Hear My People"/"Dub"	:nhs36
05.11.01	High Contrast "Make It Tonight"/"Mermaid Scar"	:nhs37
03.12.01	Delta "Submerged"/"Roots"	:nhs38

www.hospitalrecords.com
telephone : 020 7386 8760 / fax : 020 7381 8014 / e-mail : info@hospitalrecords.com

HOSPITALITY NO HOSTILITY

Hospitality at Herbal was blessed with the carousel-projector genius of Jim 'Hairy Eye' Eaton, our first real 'VJ'.

H
O S
PITA
LRECO
DSATHE
RBALEVERY
THIRDFRIDAY
*

HOSPITAL
D&B

HOSPITAL
ITY

Herbal

Herbal

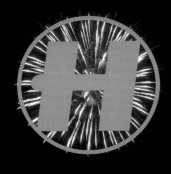

Herbal flyers, 2006-7

Travellin' Man | 8-Bit Blues →

NHS0099
SYNCOPIX

***

H
HOSPITAL

H
Krankenhaus / NHS
City·Karte · Zone 000 HVV

4 — U Schlump- U Osterstr
Eidelstedt, Wildacke
5 — Rathausmarkt - Si
U Niendorf M. -
37 — Bahnhof Altona
Osdorf – Schene
109 — Rathausm.-Harv
Winterhude, U A
120 — Roth
Alt
124 —

syncopix

Roland Syncopix was a frequent
guest at Herbal, resident at
Hospitality in Berlin, maker of
champion fun music and all round
top chap.

A mainstay of Hospital's Plastic
Surgery, Weapons and Sick
albums, he also had a few singles
on the labels over the years; most
fitting was 'General Hospital',
a track we absolutely had to
release!

HOSPITAL

going live

In 2003, Tony took London Elektricity solo,
then turned it into a totally live band.

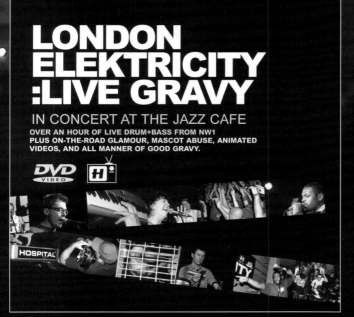

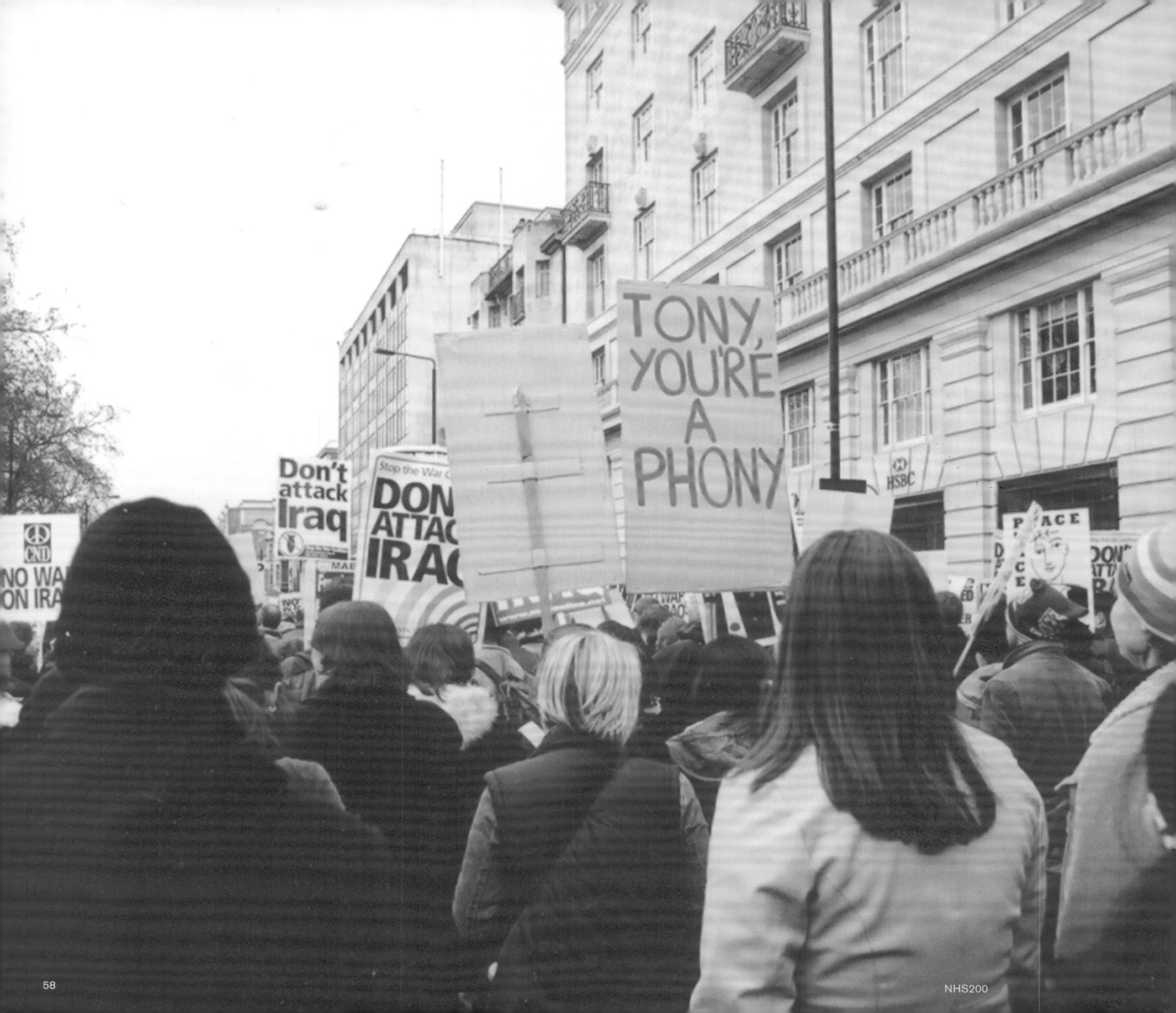
Don't attack Iraq
TONY, YOU'RE A PHONY
HSBC
CND

'Gravy' was followed up in 2005 by 'Power Ballads'.

2003 saw the release of Billion Dollar Gravy. The album photography was captured by Gry Garness at the anti-war protest in the early Spring.

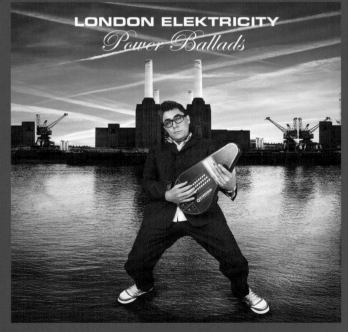

M*A*S*H01A

SOCIAL SECURITY PRESENTS:
CHILD SUPPORT
TWIN PEAKS

WRITTEN & PRODUCED BY INDUJEANE ALI LATIF. PROBABLY!
PUBLISHED BY SONGS IN THE KEY OF KNIFE / WESTBURY MUSIC.
ALL RIGHTS RESERVED. MADE IN ENGLAND.
(P)+(C) HOSPITAL RECORDS LIMITED 2003.
WWW.HOSPITALRECORDS.COM

M*A*S*H02A

SYNCOPIX
SOUL SECURE

WRITTEN & PRODUCED BY ROLAND BOSDIAHN.
PUBLISHED BY SONGS IN THE KEY OF KNIFE / WESTBURY MUSIC.
ALL RIGHTS RESERVED. MADE IN ENGLAND.
(P)+(C) HOSPITAL RECORDS LIMITED 2003.
WWW.HOSPITALRECORDS.COM

M*A*S*H03A

KONSTA
FLIRT

WRITTEN & PRODUCED BY KONSTA MIKKONEN.
PUBLISHED BY SONGS IN THE KEY OF KNIFE / WESTBURY MUSIC.
ALL RIGHTS RESERVED. MADE IN ENGLAND.
(P)+(C) HOSPITAL RECORDS LIMITED 2003.
WWW.HOSPITALRECORDS.COM

M*A*S*H04A

SOCIAL SECURITY PRESENTS:
CRISIS LOAN
ICE SCREAM

WRITTEN & PRODUCED BY MOHAMMED ALI LATIF.
PUBLISHED BY SONGS IN THE KEY OF KNIFE / WESTBURY MUSIC.
ALL RIGHTS RESERVED. MADE IN ENGLAND.
(P)+(C) HOSPITAL RECORDS LIMITED 2003.
WWW.HOSPITALRECORDS.COM

M*A*S*H05A

SOCIAL SECURITY PRESENTS:
CHILD SUPPORT
LONDON ZOO

WRITTEN & PRODUCED BY MOHAMMED ALI LATIF.
PUBLISHED BY SONGS IN THE KEY OF KNIFE / WESTBURY MUSIC.
ALL RIGHTS RESERVED. MADE IN ENGLAND.
(P)+(C) HOSPITAL RECORDS LIMITED 2003.
WWW.HOSPITALRECORDS.COM

M*A*S*H06A

SOCIAL SECURITY PRESENTS:
CRISIS LOAN
CAPED CRUSADER

WRITTEN & PRODUCED BY MOHAMMED ALI LATIF.
PUBLISHED BY SONGS IN THE KEY OF KNIFE / WESTBURY MUSIC.
ALL RIGHTS RESERVED. MADE IN ENGLAND.
(P)+(C) HOSPITAL RECORDS LIMITED 2003.
WWW.HOSPITALRECORDS.COM

M*A*S*H07A

RADAR
FIERCE FUNK

WRITTEN & PRODUCED BY PETE WEAVER.
PUBLISHED BY SONGS IN THE KEY OF KNIFE / WESTBURY MUSIC.
ALL RIGHTS RESERVED. MADE IN ENGLAND.
(P)+(C) HOSPITAL RECORDS LIMITED 2003.
WWW.HOSPITALRECORDS.COM

M*A*S*H

LOGISTICS
UPROCK

WRITTEN & PRODUCED BY KURT GRAHAM.
PUBLISHED BY ALWAYS IN THE KEY OF KNIFE / WESTBURY MUSIC.
ALL RIGHTS RESERVED. MADE IN ENGLAND.
(P)+(C) HOSPITAL RECORDS LIMITED 2003.
WWW.HOSPITALRECORDS.COM

M*A*S*H
09

a moment for m*a*s*h

M*A*S*H was a sister label dispatched in 2003 on some more dancefloor-oriented excursions. It never really picked up traction, and one last reinvention when Ricky Trickartt joined Hospital didn't pick up the desired steam either, so it was decommissioned in 2005. We still like the designs though!

purple gates

In 2005 the Hospital crew moved south of the river to The Purple Gates, setting up shop in a former old peoples' home in Forest Hill.

LENNY FONTANA presents **BLACK SUN**
SPREAD LOVE
DRUM+BASS REMIXES
NU:TONE
CHILD SUPPORT
HOSPITAL RECORDS
CATALOGUE NO: NHS64 / BARCODE NO: 666017073163

SEBA AND PARADOX MOVE ON

"GENERAL" HOSPITAL

SYNCOPIX

WWW.HOSPITALRECORDS.COM

 79

WE ARE NOW
ILL LOGIC+RAF

NHS200

gone to heaven

The first big step for Hospitality was making the trip to the West End's Heaven, becoming a quarterly residency at the club. One of the spiritual birthplaces of rave music back in the early 90s, the move initially raised a few eyebrows, and we were indebted to a young Sarah Libretto for taking a chance on us!

The 'lavish' Drum+Bass night's flyposter campaign made it all over the city and even made it as far as the BBC's premier soap opera EastEnders!

Heaven

HOSPITAL RECORDS PRESENTS

HOSPITALITY
RETURNS TO
HEAVEN

FRIDAY 25TH NOVEMBER 10-6AM

RONI SIZE / DJ ZINC
HIGH CONTRAST
RANDALL / Q-PROJECT
LOGISTICS/CYANTIFIC
SP:MC/MC RAGE/MC MOOSE

ROOM 2
tempo tantrum
SHUT UP & DANCE
+GUESTS
REZA / XERXES

ROOM 3
THE FUTURE SOUND OF BUDAPEST
SKC+CHRIS S.U.
DJ FLIGHT / NU:TONE
RUTHLESS+AYAH

ROOM 4
THE WAH WAH 45s FUNK+SOUL LOUNGE

TICKETS £12 IN ADVANCE / £15 DOOR / £13 NUS
HEAVEN UNDER THE ARCHES, VILLIERS ST, LONDON WC2N
3 LICENSED BARS / 2 CLOAKROOMS / HOSPITAL SHOP / SOUND : THE MIGHTY FUNCTION ONE   MORE DETAILS: 020 8613 0400 / INFO@HOSPITALRECORDS.COM
WWW.HOSPITALRECORDS.COM
ADVANCE TICKETS (+STD BOOKING FEE) : WWW.TICKETWEB.CO.UK OR CALL 08700 600100   ALSO AVAILABLE FROM WWW.HEAVEN-LONDON.COM/TICKETS
HOSPITAL RINGTONE SELECTION & MERCHANDISE RANGE HTTP://SHOP.HOSPITALRECORDS.COM

EastEnders
Tue, 25 Aug 2009
Programme Information

HOSPITALITY
AT HEAVEN
H 10 31 FWD>> WAH WAH45
24/11/06

NHS200

fallen angel

Our glory days at Heaven sadly
ended rather abruptly, following
a buyout of the club in 2008. We
had to cancel the party at late
notice and weren't even given the
chance to say goodbye.

attah snappah

When we met Andrew at Heaven, he was still shooting on film, but
capturing some great images. Since those early days, he's taken a full-
time reportage role with our events and artists.

We've worked with some other brilliant photographers through the
years too, like Gry Garness, Fiona Freund, Boris Austin and many more.
Contact details are in the back pages!

NU:TONE
THREE BAGS FULL
83

NU:TONE
THREE BAGS FULL
83

NU:TONE
THREE BAGS FULL
83

the first gresham

Dan Nu:Tone Gresham signed to Hospital in 2003 and his debut album followed two years later. We hired a NASA spacesuit from a central London film hire company and drove up to Cambridge with Gry Garness to shoot him around the University grounds.

Dan was a smash hit with all of the visiting Japanese tourists!

NU:TONE
SEVEN YEARS
MATRIX REMIX
B/W **STAY STRONG**
87

cambridge circus

Working with Nu:Tone introduced us to the rest of the 'family', particularly younger brother Matt Logistics, and the Commix trio (later duo). The FSOC idea quickly emerged, and delivered a number of classics!

Nu:Tone and Cambridge

NHS122LP

NU:TONE
BACK OF BEYOND

HOSPITAL

NU: TONE
FEATURING NATALIE WILLIAMS
SHINE IN

HOSPITAL

NU:TONE
WORDS AND PICTURES

FEATURING BEN WESTBEECH • 4HERO
NATALIE WILLIAMS • LOGISTICS • HEIDI VOGEL
STAC • LISA MILLETT • KYAN • SOPHIE PAUL

NHS200

HOSPITAL MIX
drum+bass selection.

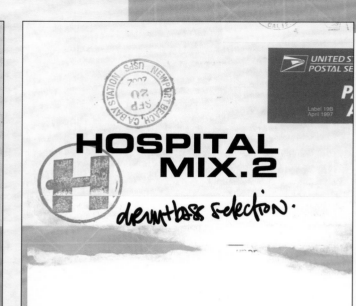

HOSPITAL MIX.2
drum+bass selection.

HOSPITAL MIX.3
drum+bass selection.
Mixed by NU:TONE

HOSPITAL MIX.4
drum+bass selection.
Mixed by CYANTIFIC

17 Baron's Court Rd
Lodon, W14 9DP
Great Britain

NHS200

nhs12lp london elektricity pull the plug

NHS19LP various artists::out patients

NHS23LP landslide::drum+bossa

NHS25 london elektricity::round the corner (original & jazztronik mix)

NHS26 london elektricity::round the corner (origin unknown mixes)

NHS30LP various artists::plastic surgery 2

NHS33LP various artists::out patients 2

NHS35 london elektricity versus robert owens::my dreams remixed by total science & high contrast

NHS40 HIGH CONTRAST::RETURN OF FOREVER / SO CONFUSED

NHS41LP HIGH CONTRAST::TRUE COLOURS

NHS43LP various artists::plastic surgery 3

NHS44R HIGH CONTRAST::GLOBAL LOVE (CALIBRE REMIX)

NHS44 HIGH CONTRAST::GLOBAL LOVE / RETURN OF FOREVER (JOHN B REMIX)

HIGH CONTRAST::RETURN OF FOREVER (LANDSLIDE REMIX)

NHS46 LONDON ELEKTRICITY::CUM DANCING / DOWN LOW

NHS47 Klute::part of me

NHS49 HIGH CONTRAST::MUSIC IS EVERYTHING > INFLUX DATUM UK REMIX / DANNY BYRD REMIX

NHS51 various artists::plastic surgery 4 #01 d.kay-dj lee / cyantific / tomahawk / zed bias

NHS53 various artists::plastic surgery 4 #02 high contrast / influx uk / zero tolerance / dj kalm+citizen feat. adam m / syncopix

NHS55 LONDON ELEKTRICITY::BILLION DOLLAR GRAVY / HARLESDEN

NHS56LP LONDON ELEKTRICITY BILLION DOLLAR GRAVY

NHS59LP VARIOUS ARTISTS::OUT PATIENTS 3

NHS62LP PHUTURISTIX::FEEL IT OUT

NHS69LP VARIOUS ARTISTS::WEAPONS OF MASS CREATION

NHS74 VARIOUS ARTISTS::FUTURE SOUND OF CAMBRIDGE EP

NHS77LP HIGH CONTRAST HIGH SOCIETY

NHS81 LOGISTICS::SPACEJAM EP

NHS84LP NU:TONE BRAVE NU WORLD

NHS88LP VARIOUS ARTISTS::WEAPONS OF MASS CREATION /TWO

NHS93 HELLO MY NAME IS Q-PROJECT

NHS95LP LONDON ELEKTRICITY POWER BALLADS

hospital mix

Started as a give-away to celebrate the launch of Hospitality at Herbal, the cut-price Hospital Mix series became an annual introduction to where the label was at, including the latest tracks with a host of exclusive future cuts in-tow too.

HOSPITALISED

CONTRAST / LONDON ELEKTRICITY / NU:TONE / LOGISTIC
JECT / CYANTIFIC / SYNCOPI

NHS100

one hundred releases and hospital art!

Hospital's tenth year in business kicked off with the label's hundredth release, 'Hospitalised' - a triple-cd set, plus a vinyl EP of brand-new collaborations between Hospital's roster. Both came packaged in a deluxe spot-varnished sleeve. Special!

The ten-years celebrations continued throughout the year, including an exhibition of ten years of Hospital covers, held at East London's Art Vinyl gallery.

the second coming of hospital mix

After ten years of Hospital and inspired by the success of Hospitality at Heaven, the Hospital Mix series was rebooted.

NHS200

HOSPITAL MIX FIVE MIXED BY LONDON ELEKTRICITY

HOSPITAL MIX.SIX MIXED BY CYANTIFIC

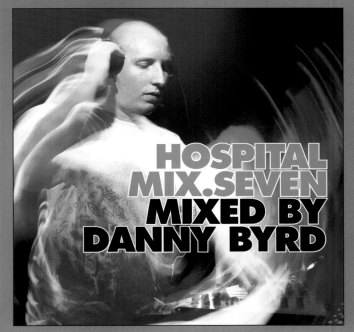

HOSPITAL MIX.SEVEN MIXED BY DANNY BYRD

HOSPITAL MIX.EIGHT MIXED BY LOGISTICS

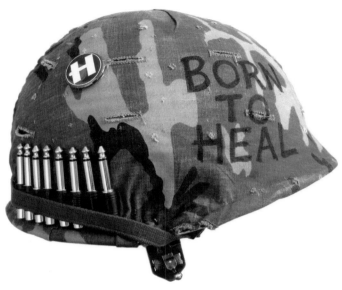

A HOSPITAL OPERATION

WEAPONS OF MASS CREATION

BORN TO HEAL

13 SEXED-UP DRUM+BASS NUGGETS FROM

**LONDON ELEKTRICITY vs NU:TONE / JOHN B / LAROQUE
DANNY BYRD+ADROK FT. MC FOXY / CYANTIFIC / LOGISTICS
SKC+BRATWA / SKC+SAFAIR / KONSTA / SYNCOPIX
NU:LOGIC / CLS+WAX / JFB**

SIDE B   7004

A: **NU:LOGIC** ON AND ON
B: **JFB** RITZ

make music not war

The spiritual successor to the 'Plastic Surgery' series came in the form of 2004's 'Weapons Of Mass Creation'. Chris' idea for the cover art was a spin on Full Metal Jacket; we had to buy an original G.I. helmet from Silvermans in Whitechapel, ask a friend's daughter to make us a badge, then stick the headphone jacks on with double-sided tape. Turned out nice though!

Volume Two was inspired by the Tamiya soldier kits. Illustrator Nick Purser was commissioned to create some unique Hospital soldiers, packing audio hardware. The bespoke NHS camo was designed by Steve 'Filthy Media' Gotts.

WEAPONS OF MASS CREATION / TWO

3xVINYL : DRUM+BASS INFANTRY ASSAULT SET

FEATURING BRAND NEW BULLETS FROM
**TOTAL SCIENCE / CONCORD DAWN / FRICTION+NU BALANCE
LOGISTICS / CYANTIFIC+TACTILE / DANNY BYRD / LAROQUE**

NHS88LP

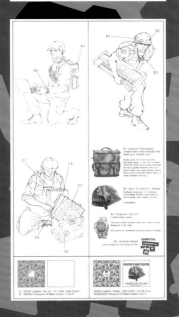

A bulk batch of the Weapons 3
patches were made especially for
the album, which were given away
with orders on the Hospital Shop

NHS200

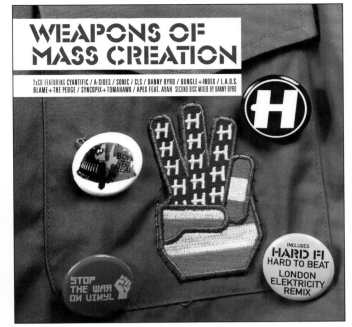

Ricky Trickartt demonstrated his Super-Badge-It operation and sewing skills for the cover of Weapons 3.

The cover art folded out into a poster on the CD edition

The series fired its parting shot in 2008 with the Friendly Fire EP.

cyantists!

Cyantific joined Hospital after a High Contrast tip-off. Originally a duo of Matt and Jon and now just Jon solo, Cyantific's music is hard to pin down, but brought a fresh lease of life to the roster.

CYANTIFIC

that side : little green men   this side : quiet star

Written & produced by Matt Whitehead & Jon Stanley. published by Songs In The Key Of Knife/Westbury Music.
Dedicated to the memory of Matthew Bird 1980-2004. Rest in peace.

Artwork by Soundadvice

71
(LC)12939

666017082813   NHS71 [P]+[C] HOSPITAL RECORDS LTD 2004

CYANTIFIC
FEATURING **DIANE CHARLEMAGNE**
DON'T FOLLOW

H 91 PULSE 101
CYANTIFIC

CYANTIFIC
that side : **output** this side : **reincarnation dub**
Written & produced by Matt Whitehead & Jon Stanley. Published by Songs In The Key Of Knife/Westbury Music.
Artwork by Soundadvice

666017095462 NH578 [P]·[C] HOSPITAL RECORDS LTD 2004

78
LC 12939

CYAN TIFIC
DISCONNECTED
B\W **THE SERPENT**

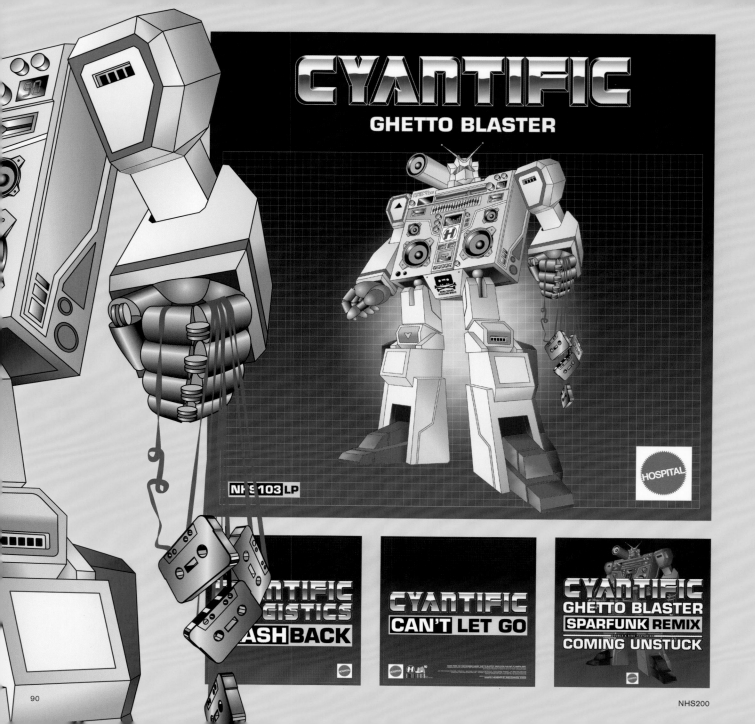

CYANTIFIC
GHETTO BLASTER

NHS103LP

HOSPITAL

CYANTIFIC LOGISTICS
FLASHBACK

CYANTIFIC
CAN'T LET GO

CYANTIFIC
GHETTO BLASTER
SPARFUNK REMIX
COMING UNSTUCK

hello

A man of porn and Porsches, Quiff AKA Q-Project proved to be quite a controversial signing to Hospital. An absolute legend in his own right as one half of Total Science, Quiff made the best party tunes around, making people move in Herbal and Heaven alike, culminating in the release of his energy-packed long-player, 'Renaissance Man'.

We made a point of getting Quiff to write his track titles in his very unique handwriting one night after his set at Herbal.

Q-PROJECT
RENAISSANCE MAN

HOSPITAL

We made pinbadges of a computerised Quiff, which we gave away at the EP launch at Herbal

Q-Project is the undisputed king of track titles, and Ricky Trickartt couldn't have been given a better one to make a cover for than 'Credit Crunch'. Ricky designed a complete cereal packet, produced a one-off box, and delivered it to Andrew Attah. The resulting image was 'directed' by Chris and Ricky for a full recession breakfast effect!

the bishi diaries

If Q-Project was considered controversial though, there aren't words to describe Mistabishi's tenure at Hospital.

Often imitated, Mista's debut single on Hospital was initially rejected by iTunes for being too blurry

The elusive NHS143 never saw an official release, but the artwork ended up being recycled for his album...

'Drop', and its predecessor 'Lean', were created by converting a digital image to analogue RF, detuning the signal, and taking a photo of the result on the screen of a ropey old TV found on a demolition site.

His album's title showed an amazing amount of foresight, as eventually he was dropped from the roster for courting controversy too many times.

Mistabishi

logging in

Music-making man-machine Logistics joined Hospital soon after his big brother Nu:Tone, and brought some self-designed sleeves with him too, setting the visual style for Logistics covers for years to come. Matt had quit his graphic design degree to take on music full-time; the artwork for 'Spacejam', 'Release The Pressure' and 'Blackout' were all Gresham originals.

NOW
MORE
THAN
EVER

can't get more
real than reality

'Now More Than Ever' was an early project at Hospital for
Ricky Trickartt, in which he proved his dedication to his art.
Following on from a Chris Goss cuepoint, Ricky decided
to construct the NMTE artwork by soldering together a
matrix of 750 LED lights, so we could physically reflect
the album name in Loggy's sunglasses. It caused Ricky
many blisters, but was worth the effort, since the real thing
looked more genuine than CGI ever would.

The Gresham family's talents don't end with Logistics either - Mr. Penfold, another Gresham brother, is a graffiti artist and illustrator, who contributed artwork to two of his brother's releases.

We found a striking image on Flickr for 'Reality Checkpoint', though it took ages to finally contact Todd and get his approval. Ricky's photoshopping skills were once again top-drawer.

The Wide Lens EP's centre labels were made by taking a photo of the type with a wide lens.

CRASH BANG WALLOP!

Loggy's third album took a turn for the arty with another unconventional
Ricky Trickartt cover. Pop Art styles!

his purple majesty

Post-it note obsessed and questionably hair-styled, Ricky Trickartt is our Rickmansworth-based one-man art department. Ricky joined Hospital in 2005, after getting his foot in the door by insulting Nu:Tone's first album cover on the internet, via the D.O.A. forum. Ever since then, his design expertise, artistic vision and unique ability with electronics, collage and home-baking have been a trademark of Hospital's growth and identity.

Logistics

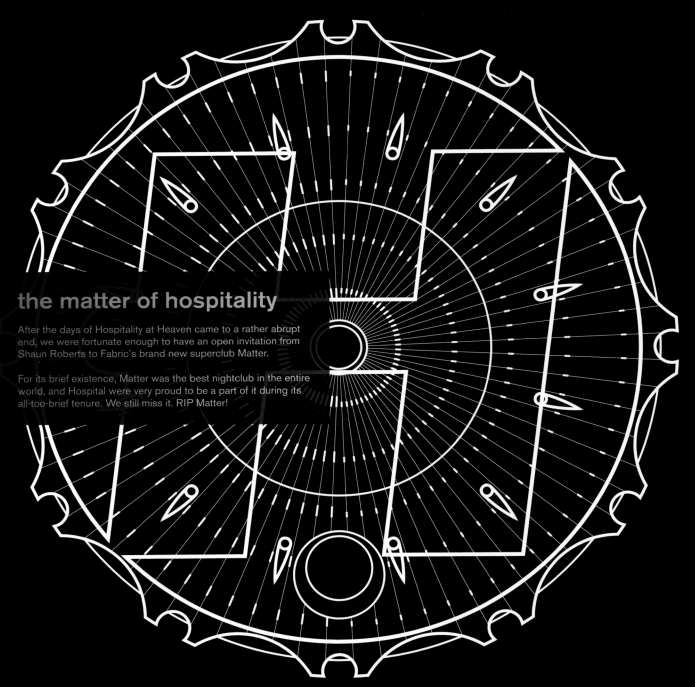

the matter of hospitality

After the days of Hospitality at Heaven came to a rather abrupt end, we were fortunate enough to have an open invitation from Shaun Roberts to Fabric's brand new superclub Matter.

For its brief existence, Matter was the best nightclub in the entire world, and Hospital were very proud to be a part of it during its all-too-brief tenure. We still miss it. RIP Matter!

surgeons' seminar

In September 2009 our friend Matt Glover, then boss at The O2's British Music Experience, invited us to hold a Q+A session on the eve of one of the now legendary Matter shows.

Hospital fans and budding music makers were given the opportunity to grill some of the producers, DJs and vocalists on the label for tips and techniques on how they make their music at this prestigious industry institution.

soft furnishings

We were lucky to have been invited to bring Hospitality to Fabric a few times over the years; notably, it's become our annual kick-off event, on the first Friday of the year. One of the most revered clubs in the world, this London clubbing institution goes from strength to strength.

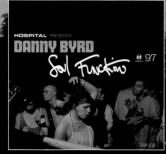

byrd grows up

Not long after signing to Hospital in 2000, the Byrd flew the nest for several years, returning in 2006 bigger, badder and with more tunes than ever, culminating in his 2008 debut album 'Supersized'. Artwork started out as a Chris Goss biro drawing, and was finally realised thanks to some CGI wizardry form designer David Hoare. Big!

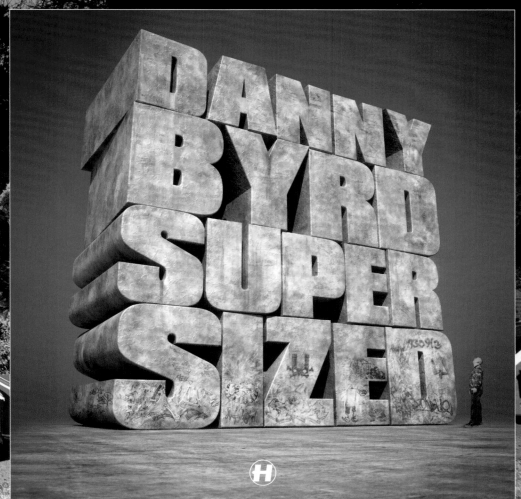

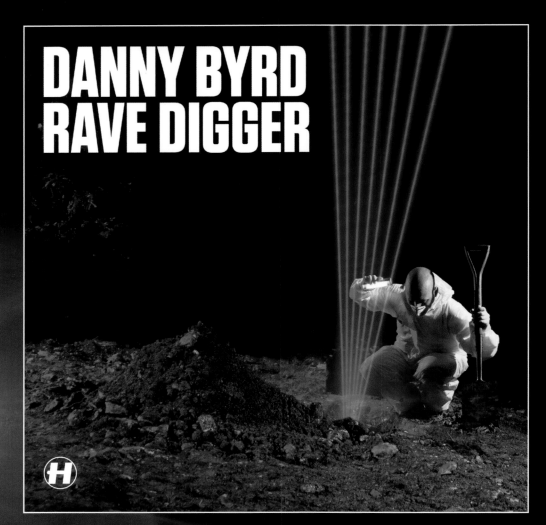

DANNY BYRD
RAVE DIGGER

Danny struck again with 2010's massive album 'Rave Digger', the lead single of which, 'Ill Behaviour', made it all the way to the UK top 40. Andrew Attah and the Byrdman went out into the woods to dig up the album cover, and the artwork spiralled from there.

The album launched at the Brixton Academy, where TVs around the venue played Rave Digger rolling news. Danny toured at Hospitality events across the country where 'Rave Digger' glowsticks and T-shirts were sold, inspiring the art for the follow-up single 'We Can Have It All'.

The project concluded with 'Tonight', another A-listed single with a video featuring an orange Danny Byrd, some pensioners and a statue of a mallard, and its cover artwork featured the heart of Hospital's operations - none other than Chris Goss' filofax!

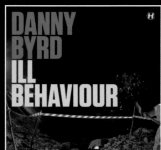

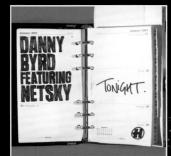

DANNY BYRD
New Album 'Rave Digger' out 11th October 2010

BYRD NEWS 11.10 HOSPITALRECORDS.COM • FOR ALL THE LATEST

the future sound of... extends its horizons

Following the success of the first 'Future Sound Of Cambridge' EP, the series extended its horizons to Budapest with SKC, Chris SU and Mindscape; Tokyo, led by T-Ak and Makoto; and in this case the outer reaches of Russia in the company of Subwave, Electrosoul System and Unquote, the latter of whom went on to join the Med School.

bratislava to brixton

Like Syncopix, another good friend of Hospital is Bratislava's B-Complex. His tune 'Beautiful Lies', from the first edition of Sick Music, rocketed out of nowhere into its position as a firm favourite of podcast-listeners and Hospitality-goers alike.

The VIP of Beautiful Lies was released as a double-A-side single along with 'Little Oranges', which according to Ricky Trickartt, is the best track title Hospital has released since 'Credit Crunch'.

Also a regular at Hospitality parties, B-Complex ensured his legendary status by having the gumption to close his set at Hospitality at Matter with John Lennon's 'Imagine', and get the entire crowd to sing along.

sick bag

'Sick Music' picked up where Weapons left off; the premium various artists selection on Hospital showcased the best of positive Drum+Bass, such as Muffler, Apex, MRSA and B-Complex!

SICK MUSIC

AGENT ALVIN • B-COMPLEX • CYANTIFIC • INFLUX UK
LONDON ELEKTRICITY + APEX • MUFFLER • RANDOMER • TOTAL SCIENCE

H
HOSPITAL

SICK MUSIC 2

B-COMPLEX
CYANTIFIC
ILLSKILLZ
MRSA

NU:TONE
RESO
SONIC
WILKINSON

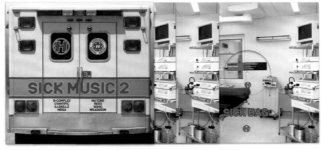
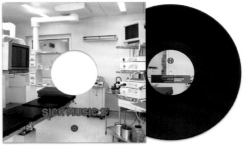

hospital mix is dead!
long live hospitality!

With Hospitality growing at a rate of knots under events manager Josh Panton, the label-oriented 'Hospital Mix' series was succeeded by a much wider Hospitality selection, featuring the best tunes from all around the bass music world, but still at a bargain price!

hospinational intertality

The spread of locations across these flyers shows some of the more outlandish places where we've been lucky enough to put on parties.

From cities like Berlin and Beijing, to Antwerp, Bern, Thorenz, Prague, and Sydney; the outernational love for Hospitality continues to spread far and wide.

It's not just an international thing either - it didn't take long to spread across our homelands too. From Exeter to Edinburgh, there aren't many cities that we haven't Hospitalised over the years!

"...and don't get me wrong, he has grown some hair"
-Grooverider, Radio 1, 2004

High Contrast returned with his second album and a whole lot of hair in 2004.

High Contrast II

'High Society's enduring image was shot on the roof of Herbal. As a firm tea-totaller, the cocktail glass was filled with cranberry juice.

The artwork for 'Tough Guys' was based on an old Italian film noir poster, in case you wondered. Lincoln worked closely with long-time friend Dave 'Droneboy' Shaw to construct the re-imagined celluloid design.

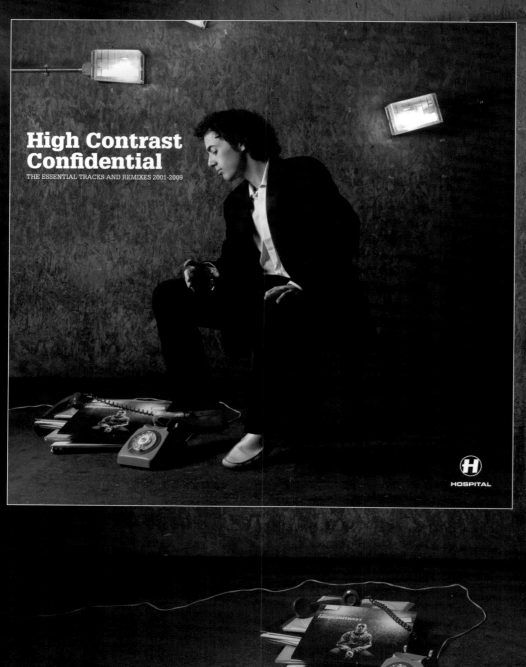

High Contrast
Confidential
THE ESSENTIAL TRACKS AND REMIXES 2001-2009

(H)
HOSPITAL

'High Contrast Confidential'
(titled as a play on 'High School
Confidential') was a kind of
greatest hits on disc one, plus
a collection of some of Link's
greatest remixes on disc two. The
cover art combined the venue of
'True Colours', the tuxedo from
'High Society', and the telephone
from 'Tough Guys'.

i'm a col-man!

Tony knew to quit when he was ahead and the band, well, disbanded after its final shows in 2006, leaving Tony sailing the London Elekship solo.

His next project was the album 'Syncopated City' which, led by the single 'Attack Ships On Fire', came in a pretty swanky deluxe 4-piece vinyl gatefold edition in 2008. The unique drawings were delivered by Stephen Walter.

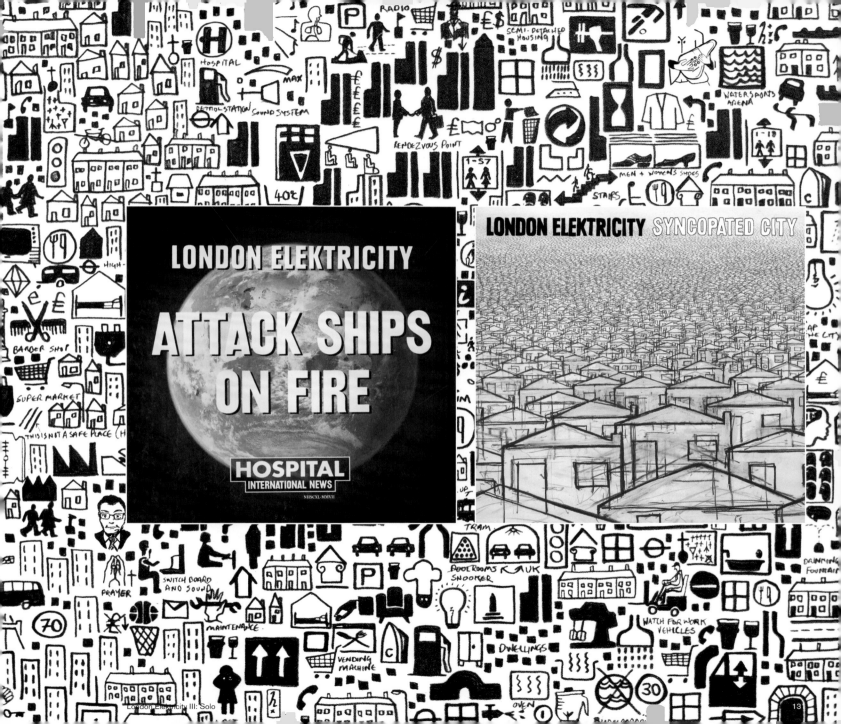

LONDON ELEKTRICITY
ATTACK SHIPS ON FIRE
HOSPITAL
INTERNATIONAL NEWS
NHSCXL-MMVII

LONDON ELEKTRICITY SYNCOPATED CITY

The multi Award-winning
HOSPITAL
PODCAST

Also on the Colmanian agenda was the Hospital Podcast, a bi-weekly podcast he has been fronting since 2006, showcasing the greatest in Drum+Bass along with questionable forays into politics, restaurant reviews and tour gossip going out directly to more than fifty thousand subscribers all around the world.

The podcast became a huge success, winning the BT DMA award for best podcast three years in a row. With more than 150 episodes clocked up in its first five years, the podcast has gone from strength to strength, and brought on its own traditions like the occasionally alarming and always entertaining annual Christmas Photoshop competiton.

Tony with Elsa Esmeralda for Hospital Podcast #142, 2011

Christmas Photoshop Competition entry 2009

LONDON
ELEKTRICITY
ELEKTRICITY
WILL KEEP
ME WARM
THE PLAN
THAT
CANNOT
FAIL

LONDON
ELEKTRICITY
FEATURING
ELSA ESMERALDA
METEORITES
DANNY BYRD
+ CUTLINE
REMIXES

LONDON ELEKTRICITY
YIKES!
REMIXES!!
S.P.Y • LOGISTICS • ENEI • LUNG

NHS191

'Syncopated City' was followed up in 2011 with 'Yikes!', an album of ginormous proportions. The album featured vocals from Elsa Esmeralda, following a successful collaboration on the track 'Just One Second' from Syncopated City.

'Yikes!' spawned two singles, no less than six animated music videos and an entire spin-off album of remixes from the latest and greatest in Drum+Bass and beyond!

med school

back to school

Hospital's Med School opened its doors in Winter 2006, and as a sister label, it has really grown into its own. Now under the management of Ash Howard, Med School has its own stable of album artists; Russia's Bop and Unquote, Joe Syntax representing South London and Lung from Cardiff.

Med School has been nuturing new artists too with its 'New Blood' album series, showcasing the greatest bass music from cutting edge artists the world over!

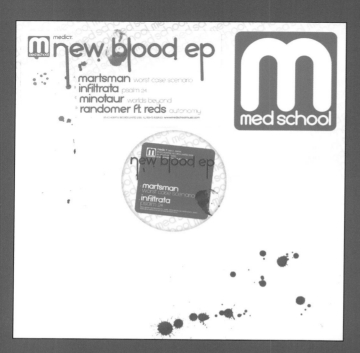

medic7.
new blood ep

martsman worst case scenario
infiltrata psalm 24
minotaur worlds beyond
randomer ft. reds autonomy

med school

new blood ep

martsman
worst case scenario
infiltrata
psalm 24

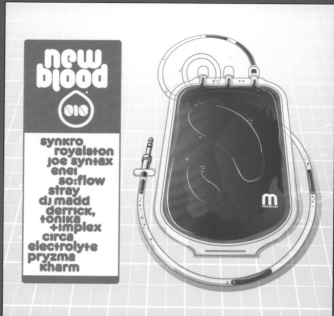

new blood

synkro
royalston
joe syntax
enei
so:flow
stray
dj madd
derrick,
tonika
+implex
circa
electrolyte
pryzma
kharm

more blood

medic 20

**stray
synkro
royalston
circa**

NEW 011 BLOOD

BASS-FILLED TONIC
FOR MIND AND BODY

med school

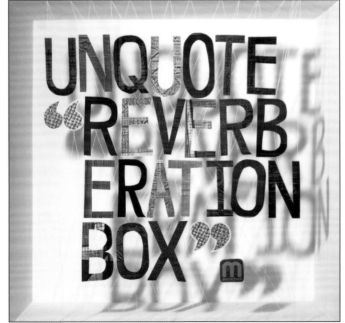

eurostar

Young Boris Daenen had only been on our radar about 6 months before we bought him a train ticket and sat down for a chat. His rise through the ranks has been rapid and meteoric. The classic Netsky jump shot was grabbed in 10minutes at City Airport by Andrew Attah on Boris' first proper visit. Look at him now!

NETSKY

calvin and klein

Reini Camo and Markus Krooked joined the Hospital family in December 2010, with their debut album dropping less than a year later. Autumn 2011 saw the C+K machine hit fifth gear with a full onslaught of audio, video and performance. At Hospitality Brixton (which doubled as the album launch party) they brought the house down when they unveiled the giant L.E.D. cage built by Justin of Meno TV with enough shock and awe to shake the floor.

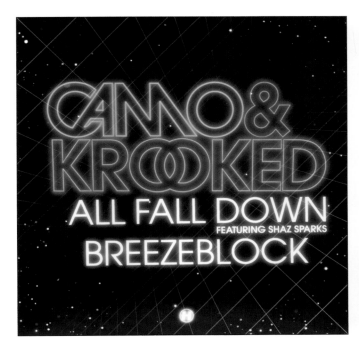

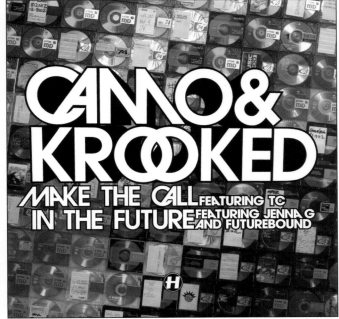

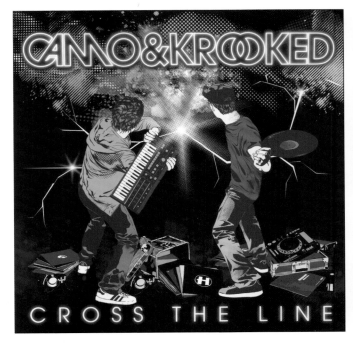

Our regular VJ, Justin Meno TV, worked night and day to develop and build this unique piece of production for the Camo+Krooked live tour.

brixton

our new London home

Brixton

Brixton

lovebox 2011

When planning our stage six months earlier,
Jools from Lovebox reassured us 'it never
rains at Lovebox'...

Brixton

155

Hospital family at the Rileys' wedding, July 2011

thanks and love:

Thank you to all our fantastic staff: Matt Riley, Zac Vibert, Edgar Dewsbery, Ash Howard, Josh Panton, Belinda Rowse, Will Weeks and Ricky Trickartt. Plus, Andrew Attah, Alex and Alex, Tom Mullet, Zac Bunce, Chimene Mohammed, Steve Wheeler, Julia Patrick, Phil Blatchford, Emily Moxon, Lucy Ambache, Chloe Straw, Adrian Bethune, and the 15 Year-strong NHS volunteer force. A huge thank you to all our families for the constant love and support.

All our artists, High Contrast, Netsky, Danny Byrd, Camo+Krooked, Nu:Tone, Logistics, Cyantific, Q-Project, Mistabishi, New Zealand Shapeshifter, and the 15 Year roll-call.

Paul Rico, Andy Slocombe, John Knight and all the SRD team, Lee Morrison and Believe Digital, Fine Tunes, Groove Attack, News, Inertia, Third Ear Japan, Central Station, Groove, Sony Office One, all the shops and retailers for keeping the faith. Westbury Music, Nichion Inc, Mushroom Music, Budde Music, and Talpa Music.

Team Hospitality: Justin Meno, Rob Stanley and Zero DB, the Hospital Street Team, and all our UK and International event partners; Tom Schroeder, Lou Putman, Nick Matthews, Claire Bewers, Pascale Duval, Dave Blackgrove, Lucinda Perkoff and the Coda family; Howard Gray, Nick Reddick, Vicki Robinson and the Reprise/Mainstage crew; Denise Melanson, Michael Cohen & AM Only New York; Shaun Roberts, Scott Patterson, and all the Fabric/Matter team, Nigel Downs, Liz Large and the Brixton O2, Sarah Libretto, Stuart Patterson, Chris and the Herbal family.

Annie Mac, Rachel Barton, Becci Abbott, James Watts, Fabio & Grooverider, Bailey, James Clark, James Forster, Dellessa James, Mistajam, Zane Lowe, Sam Rumney, Huw Stephens, Matt Fincham, Phil Stocker, Rob Da Bank, Nigel Harding, Crissy Criss, Nihal, Pete Tong, Annie Nightingale, Somethin' Else, Eddy Temple Morris, Andi Durrant, Steve O'Connor, Kmag, Trap, IDJ (RIP), DJ, Mixmag, Pete Rogers, Future Publishing, Ministry of Sound Radio, Kiss101, Groovetech, Interface, Thomas Harris, SR1/Backlash New York, FC Lokomotiv Hospital, and Hospital Bike Club.

And a big sorry to anyone we've forgotten to include. The archives have been trawled and scoured, but inevitably we will have failed on a number of points. We did our best, honest!

Chris, Tony & Tom

photographer contacts:

Andrew Attah:
www.andrewattah.com

Boris Austin:
www.borisaustin.com

Tom Chambers:
facebook.com/tcphoto

Mike Deere:
www.mikedeere.co.uk

Adrian Fisk:
www.adrianfisk.com

Fiona Freund:
www.fionafreund.com

Gry Garness:
www.grygarness.com

Mira Loew:
www.miraloew.com

Vickie Parker:
www.vickie-parker.com

Drew Ressler:
www.rukes.com

Hal Udell:
hallam@me.com

hospital staff roll-call 2011:

Tony Colman:
CEO, Artist, Licensing, A+R

Chris Goss:
Director, Label Manager, A+R

Tom Kelsey:
Director, Promotions, A+R

Zac Vibert:
Hospital Digital, Webshop

Matt Riley:
Sync Licensing, Online Promo

Ricky Trickartt:
Graphic Artist

Ash Howard:
Publishing, Med School Label Manager, A+R

Edgar Dewsberry:
Production, Licensing

Josh Panton:
Events Manager

Belinda Rowse:
Promotions Assistant

Will Weeks:
Merchandise, Webshop, A+R

credits

Identity
4, 5: Hospital, Building, EMS, Cripples and Plug logos: Chris Goss.
All other logos: Ricky Trickartt.
6, 7, 8, 9: Sleeve and label design: Chris Goss. Product photography: Ricky Trickartt.

Baron's Court
10, 11: Envelope: Mr. Scruff. Photography: Tomoko Suwa.
12, 13: Photograph: Gry Garness.

Ultrasound
14, 15: Design: Chris Goss. CD Photo: Ricky Trickartt. LE Photo: Adrian Fisk / Mixmag.

Japan
16: Photo: Ai Colman. Magazine article: Kenji Kubo. 17, 18, 19: Design: TGB. Product photography: Chris Goss. Nametag: TGB. 20: Radiotherapy: Chris Goss. Nametag: TGB. 21: Photographs: Adrian Fisk. Medkit: Sony Japan / TGB. Product photography: Ricky Trickartt.

London Elektricity I: Pull The Plug
22: Photograph: Fiona Freund. 23: Design: Chris Goss. 24: Photograph: Hal Udell. 25: Design: Chris Goss. Product photograph: Ricky Trickartt. 26: Photography: Fiona Freund. 27: Photography: Angus Macgregor.

Out Patients
29: Design: Chris Goss.
30: Artwork: Snorre Seim. Design: Chris Goss. 31: Photograph: Gry Garness. Design: Chris Goss.

Landslide
32: Photograph: Hal Udell.
33, 34, 35: Design: Chris Goss.

Plastic Surgery
36, 37: 'Plastic Surgery 2' sleeve design: Chris Goss. 'Sick Music' sleeve design: Ricky Trickartt. 'Plastic Surgery 2' Photography: Hal Udell. 38, 39: Photography: Gry Garness. Design: Chris Goss. 40: Photography: Paul Anthony. Design: Chris Goss. 41: Photograph and design: Ricky Trickartt. 42: Still from video by Conkerco. Sleeve designs: Chris Goss.

High Contrast I
43: Photograph: Dave Shaw. Design: Chris Goss. 44, 45: Sleeve designs: Chris Goss. 46, 47: Photography: Gry Garness. Sleeve designs: Chris Goss.

Herbal
48: Photograph: Jim Eaton. Design: Chris Goss. 49: Graphics: Jim Eaton, Hairy Eye. 50: Design: Chris Goss. 51: Photography: Nahush Shah, Andrew Attah. 52: Flyer designs: Ricky Trickartt.

53: Design: Chris Goss. Photography: Miguel/S2K.

London Elektricity II: Live
54, 55: Photography: Ai Colman. Design: Chris Goss. 56, 57: Photography: Andrew Attah, Ai Colman, Elio Stolz, LE Live. 58, 59: Photography: Gry Garness. Sleeve designs (except 'Hanging Rock'): Chris Goss. 'Hanging Rock' sleeve design: Ricky Trickartt.

60: MASH01-07 label designs: Chris Goss. MASH08 label design: Ricky Trickartt.

Purple Gates
61: Photograph: Ricky Trickartt.
62: Photography: Mira Loew.
63: Sleeve designs: Chris Goss.

Heaven
64-69: Flyer designs: Chris Goss. Photography: Andrew Attah, Boris Austin.

Nu:Tone and Cambridge
70, 71: Photography: Gry Garness. Sleeve designs: Chris Goss. 72: Photography: Leanne Benson. 'Future Sound Of Cambridge 1 & 2' sleeve designs: Chris Goss. 'Fututre Sound Of Cambridge 3' sleeve design: Chris Goss and Ricky Trickartt. 73: Photograph: Andrew Attah. Artwork: Ricky Trickartt. 74: Sleeve designs: Chris Goss and Ricky Trickartt. 75: Sleeve designs and cover photography: Ricky Trickartt. Nu:Tone Photograph: Andrew Attah. 76-77: Photograph: Ricky Trickartt.

Compilations I
78: Sleeve designs: Chris Goss.
79: Spines Image: Ricky Trickartt.
80: Sleeve design: Chris Goss and Ricky Trickartt. 81: Flyer design: Chris Goss and Ricky Trickartt. Photography: Art Vinyl. 82: Photograph: Andrew Attah. 83: Sleeve designs: Chris Goss and Ricky Trickartt. 'Hospital Mix 5' photograph: Drew Ressler. 'Hospital Mix 6/7/8' photographs: Andrew Attah. 84, 85: Sleeve designs: Chris Goss. Camouflage pattern: Steve Gotts. Helmet photograph: Gry Garness. Soldier illustrations: Nick Purser. Sketch: Chris Goss. 86, 87: Photography: Andrew Attah. Sleeve designs: Ricky Trickartt and Chris Goss.

Cyantific
88, 89: Photograph: Bugsy. Label designs: Soundadvice. 'Don't Follow' sleeve design: Chris Goss. 'Disconnected' sleeve design: Ricky Trickartt.
90: Sleeve designs: Ricky Trickartt. Robot illustration: Lawrence Clift, Oliver McKenna and Brian Whitehead.

Q-Project
91: Design: Chris Goss. Photograph: Andrew Attah. Graffiti writing: Q-Project. 92: Photography: Boris Austin. 'Renaissance Man' sleeve design: Chris Goss. 'Computer Love' sleeve design: Ricky Trickartt. 93: Pin badges: Ricky Trickartt. 96: Cereal box and design: Ricky Trickartt. Photography: Andrew Attah.

Mistabishi
95: Sleeve designs: Ricky Trickartt. Illustration: Unit10Collective, Guillaume Cornet, taken from 'From Memory' sleeve design and video.
96. 97: Artwork and photography: Ricky Trickartt.

Logistics
98: 'Spacejam EP', 'Release The Pressure EP' and 'Blackout': Artwork: Matt Gresham. Design: Chris Goss. 'Spacejams' sleeve design: Ricky Trickartt.
99: Logistics photograph: Boris Austin. Process and LED matrix: Ricky Trickartt. 100: Photograph: Todd S. Klassy. Illustrations: Mr. Penfold. Design and typography: Ricky Trickartt.
101: Artwork: Ricky Trickartt.
102: Artwork and design: Ricky Trickartt. Photography: Andrew Attah.

103: Desk photo: Ricky Trickartt. Ricky Trickartt photo: Andrew Attah.

Matter and Fabric
104: Design: Ricky Trickartt.
105: Photograph: Vickie Parker.
106, 107: Photography: Vickie Parker, Andrew Attah. 108, 109: Photography: Andrew Attah. Flyer designs: Ricky Trickartt.

Danny Byrd
110, 111: Photograph: Andrew Attah. Sleeve designs (except 'From Bath With Love'): Chris Goss. 'Supersized' CGI Artwork: David Hoare. 'From Bath With Love' sleeve design: Ricky Trickartt.
112, 113: Design: Ricky Trickartt. Photography: Andrew Attah. Still taken from 'Tonight' video by Burning Reel Productions.

Compilations II
114, 115: Illustrations: Ricky Trickartt. 'Future Sound Of Budapest' and 'Future Sound Of Tokyo' sleeve designs: Chris Goss. 'Future Sound Of Russia' sleeve design: Ricky Trickartt. 116: Photograph: Andrew Attah. Sleeve designs: Ricky Trickartt. 117: Sleeve design: Ricky Trickartt and Chris Goss. 118, 119: Design: Ricky Trickartt. 120, 121: Photography: Andrew Attah. Sleeve designs: Ricky Trickartt.

High Contrast II
125: Photograph: Dave Shaw.
126: Sleeve designs: Chris Goss. Photography: Gry Garness. 127: 'Tough Guys Don't Dance' artwork: Dave 'Droneboy' Shaw. 'If We Ever', 'Everything's Different' and 'Kiss Kiss Bang Bang' artwork: Ricky Trickartt. 128: 'High Contrast Confidential' photography: Cleveland Aaron. Design: Ricky Trickartt. 129: Sleeve designs: Ricky Trickartt.

London Elektricity III: Solo
130: Photograph: Drew Ressler. 131: Illustrations: Stephen Walter. Sleeve designs: Ricky Trickartt.
132, 133: Photography: Ricky Trickartt. Photoshop entry: ?.
134: Photography and illustration: Ricky Trickartt. 135: Design: Ricky Trickartt. 'Elektricity Will Keep Me Warm' image taken from the video by Rob Wicksteed. 'Meteorites' image taken from the video by Kenny Frankland.

Med School
136: Design: Ricky Trickartt. 137: 'Scapegoat' sleeve design: Chris Goss and Ricky Trickartt. 'Lifeforms' artwork: Lonekink. 'Remix Your Mind', 'Signal Drop' and 'Cerulean Blue' sleeve designs: Ricky Trickartt. 'The Amazing Adventures Of One Curious Pixel' illustration: Igor Yanovsky. 138: 'New Blood EP', 'More Blood 010' and 'New Blood 011' sleeve designs: Ricky Trickartt. 'New Blood 010' artwork: Lonekink. 'New Blood 011' cover photo: Mike Deere. 139: 'Song About My Dog' and 'Clear Your Mind' artwork: Ithinkitsnice. 'Hide Your Tears Because We Are In Heaven' and 'Reverberation Box' artwork: Ricky Trickartt.

Netsky
140-143: Photography: Andrew Attah, except 142: Top photo: Tom Chambers.

Camo+Krooked
144: Photography: Andrew Attah.
145: Sleeve designs: Ricky Trickartt. 'Cross The Line' Illustrations: Toby Whitebread. 146, 147: Photography: Andrew Attah.

Brixton and Festivals
148, 149: Photography: Andrew Attah.
150, 151: Photography, Andrew Attah and Tom Chambers.
152, 153: Photography: Andrew Attah.

156: Photograph: Andrew Attah.

159: CGI Artwork: David Hoare.